T0208726

YOUR GUARDIAN ANGEL'S

GUIDE TO

HOSPITALS

[FUNNY AND NOT-SO-FUNNY TALES FROM BED #1111]

WRITTEN BY
STACEY FRIEDLANDER

EDITED BY
ILENE LEVENTHAL

iUniverse, Inc.
New York Bloomington

iUniverse books may be ordered through booksellers or by contacting:

iUniverse
1663 Liberty Drive
Bloomington, IN 47403
www.iuniverse.com
1-800-Authors (1-800-288-4677)

Because of the dynamic nature of the Internet, any Web addresses or links contained in this book may have changed since publication and may no longer be valid. The views expressed in this work are solely those of the author and do not necessarily reflect the views of the publisher, and the publisher hereby disclaims any responsibility for them.

ISBN: 978-1-4502-6735-9 (sc)
ISBN: 978-1-4502-6736-6 (ebook)

Printed in the United States of America

iUniverse rev. date: 10/20/2010

To Stacey's loving and devoted parents
Arlene and Steve Friedlander

Acknowledgements

Our special thanks to George Nicholas for his guidance.
Our heartfelt appreciation to Jon Hueber for his
continued support and encouragement.

Table of Contents

Preface from Jillian

Dear Readers and Friends,

My sister, Stacey Lynn Friedlander, the author of this humorous yet informative book, died on April 26, 2004. She was 41 years old. Her death was sudden and tragic.

Stacey was the most creative person I have ever known. Whenever I hear the term "thinking outside the box", I cannot help but visualize my sister. Through her work as an advertising executive and in her everyday life with her friends and family, my sister never ceased to amaze us all with her creative talents and unique ideas. She was known in her field for her hard work, diligence, dedication to her clients, and for always coming up with an extraordinary idea…that was Stacey…and nobody, I mean nobody, could plan a party like my sis!

My sister lived her life to the fullest for many years. Creativity was certainly her gift but she will also be remembered for her humor, positive energy and her great big hearty laugh. Stacey laughed a lot, smiled a lot and as life became painful, she cried a lot.

Stacey was addicted to pain killers and suffered much the last few years of her life. She made several attempts to detox and live a healthy life but unfortunately that never happened.

Four years before her death, Stacey was in a terrible car accident which led to many hospital stays, many surgeries and too many medications.

After Stacey's death, I found her "memoirs" tucked away in her apartment. Along with her journals, pictures of her family and cards from her nieces and nephews, was the outline and notes for this book. It was a year before I was able to read what Stacey had written. I laughed and cried as I read about her journey of life and her entrance to death.

Stacey had a way of hiding her internal struggles and pain. After reading her journals and this book, it became clearer to me just how difficult her life had been.

Even through her darkest hours, Stacey was always there to lend a hand, to lend her heart. She told me about her idea of a hospital book during one of our hospital visits. She wanted to help others through this treacherous and painful process. That was Stacey; no matter what life brought her, she found a way to smile and a way to help others.

When I found the book I sent it to my Aunt Ilene, who was very excited to edit Stacey's work. Stacey and Aunt Ilene always shared a connection (more than just hospital visits!) and I knew she would be the person to get this book published. Her persistence, patience and love are integrated into my sister's journey and throughout this book.

I miss my sister everyday. As the sixth anniversary of her death is approaching , I still cannot believe that this vivacious, talented woman, who loved and was loved so deeply, is no longer with us. I often feel Stacey's presence, her energy and her pain.

This book is the essence of my sister. It is what I want people to remember about her...her light, her humor, her creativity and her passion to help others, even in her darkest hours. This, I believe, is Stacey's legacy.

Introduction

Okay, you're thinking "how can you be my guardian angel, you don't even know me? Why you?"

A skeptic! We're kindred spirits already. But you do make excellent points. Let me answer the second question first. *Why me?* Because I spent an inordinate amount of time in hospitals. That's it, pure and simple.

I didn't choose to do so. Believe me, I'd rather have spent that time sitting under an umbrella on a tropical beach holding a drink with its own little umbrella. But I didn't have a choice.

However, unlike a lot of people, I was awake and lucid throughout most of that time. And I observed. And through plenty of trial and error, I learned things that made my time there a little more tolerable.

You're likely reading this because you or a loved one soon won't have a choice but to take an address that's a bed number. It won't be a picnic, but it can be a little more, maybe even a lot more, tolerable.

Now to the first question: *"How can I be your guardian angel when I don't even know you?"* Well the hospital doesn't know you either. In fact, hospitals are based on the idea that they don't have to "know" you, that every "you" is basically the same.

We are all a bunch of organs wrapped inside the biggest organ of all and given some structure by bones—all of which, organs and bones, are supposed to be virtually the same in everyone (I'm leaving gender out of this for the moment). Only in the case of you and me and anyone else in a hospital bed, one or more of those organs aren't working as they should; one or more of those bones are broken. The hospital's goal is to make us just like everyone else again, so there really isn't anyone to "know"—we're all supposed to be exactly the same. That's *hospital* success.

To do so, there are procedures and rules and methodologies, and, because hospitals are businesses, too, there are also efficiencies. Those are created by people divorced from patient care that obsess about ways to deliver that care in the least costly way—once again based on the idea that we are basically interchangeable. After all, doesn't that happen every day? The bed numbers stay the same, but there's a new person. Same IV stand and way to put the needle in. Same charts. Same lingo.

It's easy to feel instantly lost when you become part of a big, rolling system. But the very thing that makes the situation so trying also opens a door for me to help you. I don't have to know you to help you; I only have to know hospitals and know that you're about to go into one.

If I can share what I've learned with you, you have a chance to achieve not just *hospital* success, but individual success—feeling better while you get better.

Chapter One

The dictionary tells it like it is.

pa•tient *n*: One who suffers (archaic)

Archaic, my butt. *One who suffers* is the real definition of a patient today, not the namby-pamby *"person under medical care"*.

If ever someone has earned the right to be angry, the right to protest, the right to complain, it's the patient. Annoyance? Delay? Hardship? Pain? You bet.

Yet though you've earned the right to bitch, moan and kvetch, bitching, moaning and kvetching won't work. In addition to everything else you may be dealing with, you have to play the system. And the first step to playing the system is to make the distinction between it and the people running it.

It's a hard leap to make when you're feeling completely vulnerable and at their mercy, but they're stuck in the same system you are—and most of them are in it because somewhere, in some far off idealistic time, they wandered into it because they wanted to help people like us.

Be human, engage with your caregivers. The more you give and care, the better the care you will receive.

CHAPTER TWO

Want that last Popsicle?

My Aunt Rosie always said "you catch more bees with honey". I guarantee that chocolates, cookies and particularly brownies work every time as well. Whenever a new face comes into your room as part of their job, invite them to stop by *any time* for a goodie. Their faces light up like a Christmas tree!

Night nurses are particularly fond of this, as they need a little sugar to get them through their late shift. On occasion I have even convinced the nurse's assistant who checks your blood pressure and temperature throughout the night to skip the one at 2 am. Ask friends and family to keep you well stocked; they don't want to show up empty-handed anyway. But even if you have no sweets to pass out, there's plenty you can, and should, do.

Make friends. I know you feel like hell, I mean you *are* in the hospital, but take the time to ask the nurses and techs and cleaning people their names and how they are feeling. Ask them something personal, like weekend plans or how their kids are doing in school. These are the people who are ultimately responsible for your every need.

And it's just human nature that when there's one popsicle left in the 11th floor freezer, it's going to go to the nice patient in bed 1111 who talked to Nurse Ramona about her night classes in pharmacology at Bowie State. For other *patients*, (that is, those who haven't made a personal connection, who are a category rather than a unique individual with a name) it's "sorry, we're out of popsicles."

There are varying degrees of "no more popsicles", too. Those of us who go that extra mile with Sandy, Mike and Chavonne (nurses have names, too) and ask about their sick pets and shopping trips and family visits, have earned the right to oh-so-humbly mention, "I heard they had popsicles on 12 West last night. Think there might be any left?"

Odds are pretty good that when you care and take the time, your nurses will go that extra mile for you—in this case, to the twelfth floor freezer.

Chapter Three

What to bring with you
(besides patience, good humor, a steely resolve, etc.)

We all know how to pack for a vacation. Trust me, this is completely different.

You receive a free "gift" from the hospital when you are rolled into your room. It consists of that faded pink plastic water pitcher, cup and kidney shaped thing that looks like what the dentist gives you to spit in, plus a tooth brush, tooth paste and a sand-paper box of tissues. Keep the first three, but bring all your own toiletries. Ladies, that includes lipstick to make you feel human. Also bring a t-shirt or nightgown. Don't forget your eyeglasses and a pad and pen to jot down any necessary medical information or other things you want to remember. Also, I'm a big fan of index cards (see chapter 5).

Hospitals also give you a pair of "no skid" socks that do come in handy. I have a collection of them in my sock drawer at home.

CHAPTER FOUR

You've made new friends, but bring an old one, too: your advocate.

I was once in the hospital receiving an IV block to alleviate nerve pain in my foot. As I was resting peacefully, two nurses came into my room with a gurney. Had my doctor ordered another MRI or CAT scan? As they were sliding me onto the gurney I asked: "Where are you taking me?"

"The surgical team is ready to remove your gallbladder"

Believe it or not, these "mix-ups" occur all the time. Would I have gotten all the way to surgery before the mistake was discovered? I doubt it, but I'd rather not find out—nor even be wheeled around hallways for no good reason.

Always ask questions. If you are having surgery mark the spot with a black marker --don't laugh, many wrong feet or knees or shoulders have gone under the knife mistakenly. Now, you can't be expected to practice absolute non-stop vigilance, you need help.

While you are recovering from surgery and are still a bit out of it from the anesthesia or pain medications, it is imperative that **someone be in your room with you at all times.**Their job is to check your IV and alert the nurse if it runs out.

It helps if that advocate isn't squeamish around blood, needles or urine…and I speak from experience here! Your hospital advocate can't be shy, about your body or your needs.

The advocate should check all medications that are administered. Just by having the nursing staff know that someone has that responsibility, the chances of you inadvertently getting the wrong pill already drop immediately.

Once you have recovered enough to be your own advocate, always check the pills and charts. If you are unsure of anything you have the right to refuse medication until you discuss it with your doctor. Don't be intimidated by a "bully nurse".

CHAPTER FIVE

Think in shifts

The first thing you might want to know is the Shift Changes. Typically, most hospitals have nursing staff shifts that run from 7 a.m. to 4 p.m., 4 p.m. to 11 p.m. and 11 p.m. to 7 a.m. Find out if that's the case where you are. If so, all you have to remember is 7, 4 and 11.

Don't ask for anything within 15 minutes of a shift change, before or after. And if you go ahead and do it anyway, don't be afraid to ask again when the shift change is over. Chances are your nurse has already gotten everything ready to pass the torch on to the next shift, so your request may have fallen through the cracks. Also, the incoming shift usually takes the first 15 to 20 minutes to read the charts of their assigned patients, so if it's something you need right away, don't be shy.

When your doctor visits be sure to add whatever you might need to your chart right then and there. Hand the doctor an index card with your request in writing. Too often, by the time the doctor leaves your room and gets to your chart they forget to write your request.

Even if all you need is Pepto Bismol, if it isn't on your chart in writing you won't get it until the nurse finds your doctor or the resident doctor on duty to okay it. Why not just get it done when you have his or her attention already? Even in the case of a sleeping pill, don't wait until the evening to ask for something to help you sleep. You see, by then all the docs are home doing what you're supposed to be doing, sleeping! Ask when the Docs are awake, like during the day. It may take a while for a nurse to get in touch with the Doc so he/she can write the order.

Your only sense of time (especially if you don't have a bed by the window) may be from the TV, but in hospital-world, shifts rule.

CHAPTER SIX

Color-coded price tags—with no prices on them!

All those little stickers the nurses place on your chart...consider them price tags. Each tag has an acronym of the procedure (for example, the CT in CT Scan stands for Computed Tomography), a code # and what the product actually costs as well as what *you* will be charged for it. At checkout time, your chart is scanned and BINGO, here's what you owe—and they have backup!

Remember that whatever you ask for, even if it is lotion or powder, you will be charged for it. I once asked for a band aid. The nurse was very thoughtful and brought me a handful. However, on my bill at checkout was a line item for five (rather expensive) band aids!

Some hospitals allow individuals to qualify for social assistance. Call the Benefits and Administration department of the hospital and ask what programs might be available to assist you in paying your hospital bill. You can get help even if you have insurance.

I had a PPO policy that covered 80%, which still left a sizable balance that I had to cover, an amount I knew I didn't have and knew I would not have in the near future. Although the paperwork was tedious and extensive, the end result was a $62,000 judgment in my favor. In other words, the hospital wrote off $62,000, no strings attached.

Tip: Check into Social Security Disability; find out if you qualify, how to apply and the process.

CHAPTER SEVEN

IVs: Whose arm is it anyway?

I have a rule: only two tries per nurse. After that, you ask for someone else. And no prodding or searching for the little guys.

Adopt this rule as your own; **Do Not** learn by your own experience; learn from mine. I wish someone had written a book like this so that I didn't have to learn the hard way! However, if you are getting ready to go in to the hospital and you are reading my book, then I have accomplished my goal.

You have a right to ask for an IV tech, a specialist who does far more IV work than the floor nurses. Now, I've told you to make friends with the staff, and you don't want to alienate the nurse determined to get that needle into your arm.

Be assertive, but sweet. "Don't worry, it isn't your fault, this happens to me all the time. Last time I was in the ER they couldn't get an IV started either."

The first time I needed one I thought I had to be the stoic patient. Not knowing any better, I allowed the nurse to poke and prod (stick the needle further into my vein and move it around to find the darn thing). She went back and forth from one arm to the other. I bit my lip so hard it bled. After half an hour, she reluctantly called for another nurse. She looked so dejected that I felt sorry for her; until I saw all the bruising and swelling over the next few hours. Now I know better. Those are my arms and <u>my</u> veins, and I'm sorry if they're not available for on-the-job training. Some nurses, however, are truly angels! One of those angels told me that I should always ask the nurse or tech to use a butterfly needle. She said that they are the smallest and are perfect for difficult veins. I actually hugged her!

You may be told that they don't have any butterfly needles; not true! They may not have one with them but they can ALWAYS go to the supply room if they are willing to take the time. As I said, be sweet but firm and Do Not allow them to use anything other than a butterfly needle. I thought I knew it all; boy was I wrong! The last nurse that had to take blood from my arm did use a butterfly needle. After two frustrating tries she called in another nurse who immediately said that she was going to get a <u>blue</u> butterfly needle, which was the smallest.

My mouth dropped and I swear I almost fell out of bed (I may have actually fallen if the "zoo rails" weren't up!). I now know that the butterfly needles are color coded! But are they color coded the same in every hospital? Because I seem to end up in various hospitals, depending on which of my many specialists I call, I refuse to risk it.

The first words out of my mouth when the tech enters my room are, "How are you today, do you have the smallest butterfly needle with you?", as I smile and try to look teary eyed. I've seen some strong and controlling personalities turn to pudding when it comes to doctors and nurses. IVs are just one example. Remember, while being in the hospital is essentially giving over control to others, knowing that you do have rights, that there are limits and it's still *your* body, can be a major source of comfort.

CHAPTER EIGHT

Visitors, part 1—a chance to kvetch

At least every conversation I had with another patient in the hospital eventually got around to the subject of the competence, or lack thereof, of the hospital staff.

Now, I know I spent a chapter telling you to make friends with the staff, and I meant it. Seeing them as people helps remind them to see you as a person, too, and not just a chart. But don't you sometimes want to slap even your best friends? And don't they often deserve it? It takes work to keep up a relationship, even when you're feeling 100%. And as you may have noticed by now, I'm no Pollyanna—there are some people you'll never be friends with, and that's okay. So it's also okay to vent about the inevitable mess-ups and bad care. As a matter of fact, it can even be healthy in some forms. Visitors give you the chance to do so. Just don't do it in the presence of a hospital employee or attending doc. If you're going to complain, pull the door closed. Then go ahead and vent: I repeat, *just don't do it in the presence of a hospital employee or attending doc.*

Even if you think the little cleaning woman in the corners english isn't up to understanding the colloquial use of the term "brain-dead", refrain from saying anything bad about your caregivers until everyone in the room with you is on your team (i.e.,; not a hospital staffer.) Just as in football, you never give the other team your playbook. Even if everything you say is totally justified, when passed around second-hand as "what you've said", the next time you get that IV nurse with the gentle touch you get along with so well, she may have lost her gentle part!

CHAPTER NINE

Visitors, part 2—good things come in small doses

So, what *do* you talk about? Let the visitors do a lot of the talking. And I mean talk, not cross-examine. After all, you're exhausted, you're depressed, you look like hell, how are you going to answer, "How ya doing?" What's up? Anything new?" Believe me, having to repeat the same thing about your health over and over again can be very wearing. The best thing a visitor can do is take up the conversational slack and help take the patient's mind *away* from what is all around him or her the whole time the visitor isn't there.

If you have a visitor that simply can't do that, who is making you do more work than you have the energy to offer, there's nothing wrong with sending a few subtle clues to the effect that you're not ready to do your part—like falling asleep. And yes, I mean faking it. Close your eyes. Breathe deeply. The visitor will gladly leave knowing they've done their part and left you in a good place.

If that sounds too deceptive for you, consider this: as soon as you've checked in, you've left your privacy at the door. You get visitors at visiting hours, no matter how *you* feel at the time. And if you need something done to you or need help going to the bathroom while you have a visitor, well, there you are. I say that making the most of the little control you do have is nothing to be ashamed of. Don't be coy. Ask your visitors to please step outside for a few minutes. That will usually elicit an "I've got to run anyway" –if it doesn't, they can hang out in the hall for a few minutes.

TIP TO VISITORS: Create a list of things to talk about. Be upbeat and happy, but don't overdo it; you don't want to leave the patient more depressed by your fabulous life. Here are some good choice topics to discuss: sports, neighborhood gossip, kids' school projects, last argument with your spouse, recent Oprah episodes. Remember, you've already shown you care simply by being there. Help in the way the patient needs help, even if that means leaving.

Chapter Ten

Hospital Cuisine

Three meals a day; no food shopping, no cooking, no cleaning up and your meals are even served to you in bed! How great is that? Wipe that smile off your face and think again. While the idea sounds enticing, let's get real... The hospital kitchen has to turn out hundreds of meals to be served at the same time three times a day seven days a week. So, if you are expecting a hot home cooked meal, forget it! In the hospital's defense, they are constantly trying to improve on the quality of their food and the service they provide. Did you know that in many hospitals you can pick up your phone and call food service? You may be able to order something that is not on the daily menu and if you are served something you didn't order they will make sure you get what you ordered. Remember, it never hurts to ask but don't get all up in their face about it, watch the attitude! My Aunt Rosie always said," You can catch more bees with honey!"

Like the hospital food or not, I admit that checking off the little box next to the "food of choice" on tomorrow's menu, is sometimes the highlight of my otherwise boring day. In fact, the first thing I look for when the tray is slapped down in front of me is the next day's menu. How lame is that?! If you don't see the darn thing, just lift up your plate.Yes, that gravy stained white sheet of paper sticking to your plate affords you the opportunity to make choices. Don't forget to fill it out and give it to the food service person who collects your tray.

It sucks if you forget because the kitchen will decide what to serve you and believe me, it won't be a pleasant surprise! It's challenging enough to identify the food served to you even if you do remember what you ordered. Your plate is like a run-on-sentence, where do the mashed potatoes and gravy end and the slices of turkey begin???

There is much to be said about hospital cuisine; some good and some bad, depending on the hospital. Here are just a few things that bug the ----- out of me:

1. eggs that taste like rubber made out of some synthetic powder

2. toast that is covered with plastic wrap to keep it warm but actually produces cold soggy toast

3. gravy with big lumps in it

4. mashed potatoes that are so dry they stick to the roof of your mouth

5. green Jell-O (who likes green Jell-O anyway?)

6. being served an "early bird special" dinner at 5 o'clock knowing full well that starvation sets in again at 9 pm

My list goes on and on so my advice to you is to make lemonade out of lemons. Don't be shy! When someone asks if there is anything they can bring you, step up to the plate and ask for that deli tuna on rye with chips and a pickle. Visitors never come empty handed so you might as well be honest and tell them what you really want. Open your mouth; this is not the time to be polite. Actually, you will be doing them a favor because they will feel really good about "saving the day" so it's a win win situation!

Oh, yes, do bring a magic marker to the hospital with you. It is important to clearly label your food with your name and room number before you ask the nurse to put it in the refrigerator until you are ready to eat it. In case you don't already know, there is a patient's refrigerator on every floor so take advantage of it.

Don't confuse room service in a hotel with room service in a hospital! If you do, you are in for a rude awakening! Speaking of "awakening", while in the hospital you will never get a decent nights sleep due to the annoying nurse that keeps popping in throughout the night to take your vital signs. Just when you are finally in the midst of a hot dream where you are on a Hawaiian island sipping a margarita and about to grab the butt of some gorgeous hunk that has been drooling over you all day, you are abruptly brought out of your reverie by the A.M. nurse whose shift has just begun.

The light is switched on and a voice pierces through the room, "Hi, my name is Marianna", as she scribbles her name on the chalkboard hanging on the wall in front of you. "I will be your nurse for today" she says cheerfully. Sure, your own private nurse... just try pushing the call button and see how long it takes Miss Marianna to remember that you are her patient! Now you are really pissed because it is much too early for a "meet and greet" not to mention the demise of that steamy dream you were so in to! But she is only doing her job so just go with it.

Once your nurse finally completes her morning routine and leaves your room, you decide to brush your teeth, comb your hair and try to look half human. After all, the nice clean sheets and pillowcase that were left on the chair will soon be put on your bed so you might as well be as fresh as they are! Then, suddenly you hear that familiar sound of wheels turning and screeching to a halt. Before you have a chance to move, a tray of "whatever" is placed before you.

Ready or not, here it is!!! Timing in life is everything. When you are in the hospital you might as well forget that. Like it or not, your meals are a scheduled event. If you decide to wait before consuming, the hot will get cold and the cold will get hot so "bib up" my friend! I already told you how annoying your 5 o'clock "dinner is served" meal is. Unless you are an octogenarian you had better have a plan in place when, around 9 pm, your stomach lets you know it is not very happy by a loud "FEED ME" roar. Now is the time to reach for that stash and by all means, DO NOT count calories while you are in the hospital! If you want to reach for that box of Russell Stover chocolates then go for it! You deserve some immediate gratification. I always say, "Don't put off until tomorrow what you can eat today!"

LAST CHAPTER

Unfinished Symphony

Sadly, this book is unfinished. Much like Stacey's life, there are missing chapters. However, she did write an outline of the chapters she intended to complete. We decided to include her chapter headings in hopes that you will use your imagination to "read between the lines". In life and even beyond, Stacey continues to inspire us with her wisdom and creativity. She is your guardian angel in bed # 1111.

ADDITIONAL CHAPTER HEADINGS FOUND IN STACEY'S NOTES

Television: seek no answers here.
What not to watch when you're trying to recuperate, and why.

Physical therapists: why they're always smiling.
The short answer is: they're not the ones in pain. And while you may want to strangle them for being so cheerful, the demeanor and the treatment, both work.

Attending to your Attending: lists are your friends.
Why you need to prepare to talk to your own doctor every day; and another reason I suggest you pack note cards and pens.

PCAs: are you really in control?
Drugs on demand, sort of.

Treasured Moments in Stacey's Life

Stacey (age 10)

Stacey (age 4) and brother Andy (age 2)

Stacey, Andy and cousin Amon in Florida visiting grandparents

Stacey with immediate family at summer home,
"kdb" in Shadyside, Maryland, 1982

Stacey with brother Andy, and sister Jillian on summer cruise

Stacey with Dad

Stacey with parents, siblings and grandparents
From Left Top Row: brother-in-law Scott, Jillian, Mom, Dad, and sister-
in-law Tracey Andy, Pop and Gram Diener, Stacey and Pop Friedlander

Stacey with Aunt Suki, Gram Diener and Mom

Stacey with Pop and Gram Friedlander in the South
of France, one of Stacey's favorite spots

Stacey with Diener Family, From Left Top Row:
Suki, Dad, Mom, Andy, nephew Jeremy, niece Alexis,
Pop, Gram, nephew Danny, Amon, Uncle Russell, Tracey,
nephew Kade, Stacey, nephew Jack, niece Kayla, Jillian,
nephew Ethan, cousin Minh, Scott, and nephew Nicolas

Stacey and Aunt Ilene

Stacey and Mom

Stacey, Jillian and Mom

Stacey with Aunt Rose

Stacey at Canyon Ranch Spa with the girls
From Left, Top Row: cousin Jody, Aunt Sydney,Gram, cousin Felicia,
Aunt Ilene, Aunt Phyllis, Mom, Suki, Jillian, Aunt Barbara, cousin Lisa

Stacey out on the bay with Maxine Siegel

Stacey with long time friend, Cindy Kolker Shuman

Stacey with dear friend, Dara Schain Feldman

Stacey partying with Mike Sadow

Stacey's graduation from Rollins College, 1984

Stacey promoting a new shopping outlet

Stacey in the South of France

Stacey's beloved dog, Sydney

Stacey Lynn Friedlander was born in Potomac, Maryland. She graduated from Rollins College in 1984 with a Bachelor of Arts Degree in English. Stacey then obtained her real estate license but felt she wanted to follow a more creative path. She was hired by Earl Palmer Brown Advertising Agency where she worked as an account executive.

Stacey continued to look for an even greater challenge. She found her niche in advertising at Henry J. Kaufman and Associates in Washington, DC. Stacey's skill sets and genial nature along with her unique creativity earned her quick ascent to Director of Promotions at Kaufman and Associates. She enjoyed traveling the United States representing and promoting MacArthur Glen outlet centers. Stacey then founded Friedlander Promotions, which was the culmination of her hard work and stellar reputation. Stacey was a highly regarded advertising and promotions executive. She possessed a talent for creativity and organizational skills. Stacey believed in hard work and nothing less than perfection.

Jillian Copeland, Stacey's younger sister, grew up in Potomac, MD. The sisters came from a tight knit family including their brother, Andy, and parents, Steve and Arlene Friedlander (plus a few dogs along the way). Their childhood was loving, memorable and happy.

Jillian, and her husband Scott Copeland, now have four thriving sons. Nicolas, their third, has many special needs; to help meet them, Jillian and Scott founded a school where "Nicol" could develop and thrive. Jillian is now the full-time Director of *The Diener School* also located in Potomac, MD. Today, *The Diener School* serves over 35 students grades K-5 with various sensory, learning and language needs.

Jillian was inspired by all of her family members including Stacey, who volunteered for several community organizations. Philanthropy and community service has always been naturally woven into their lives. Jillian is proud to be giving back to her community. She continues to hope that the special education she is fortunate to be able to give her son will be available to many other children in the years to come.

Ilene Leventhal is a native Washingtonian. She was born to Rose and Julius Epstein in 1945. As a teen, Ilene volunteered for many years at The Children's Convalescent Home and Saint Elizabeth's Hospital, both located in DC. Ilene graduated from American University with a B.A. in Education. She then married and taught first grade in New Haven, Connecticut. After having three children, Ilene volunteered for numerous local organizations. Ilene founded and was Director of her own non-profit charity, HAND TO HAND. Their goal was to assist homeless individuals and "working poor" families in the Washington Metropolitan area. Founded in 1990, HAND TO HAND became one of the most successful local charitable organizations in its field.

Recognized for her important work and dedication to the community, Ilene was named Potomac Citizen of the Year in 1995 and a Washingtonian of the Year in 1999. The Governor of the State of Maryland, the Maryland State Senate and its House of Delegates also honored her. Additional recognition for her work through HAND TO HAND was received from Head Start, Hadassah, March of Dimes and the Daughters of the American Revolution, among others.

In July 2001, HAND TO HAND was merged into Community Ministries of Montgomery County, which has since changed its name to Interfaith Works. The HAND TO HAND eviction prevention program (Project: Safety Net) continues to thrive under the Interfaith Works umbrella. Ilene now serves as an advisor for HAND TO HAND and is involved in fundraising for the continued success of Project Safety Net.

SHARED MEMORIES OF STACEY

Susan's Memory

I was Stacey's occupational therapist. I mainly did range of motion exercises for her arm. She experienced a tremendous amount of pain during therapy but always wanted to push through it to finish her therapy sessions. Stacey was highly motivated to get her life back. I did not know Stacey before the accident but we became great friends while she was in the hospital. Stacey and I also talked on the phone after she was discharged.

Stacey had been my patient for a few weeks when she shared the details of her accident. She was very matter-of-fact about what happened and felt horrible about the worry she was causing her family. She worried about her mother all the time. I tried to always schedule Stacey when I wouldn't be rushed so we could "hang out". One day I didn't see her until almost three o'clock and she gave me hell. "What do you mean coming to see me so late? Can't you do better than this? What am I, an after-thought?". When she finally quit gripping at me, I told her to pipe down and that I saved the best for last! She laughed and quickly responded, "don't try to feed me that line of crap". Stacey always had to have the last word, usually with a big laugh.

I also remember Jill coming into the hospital with a big white coat on while she was pregnant. Stacey immediately started laughing and told Jill she looked like a big, friggin marshmallow. I laughed so hard I almost cried! Stacey was so funny, even in her darkest hour. Don't get me wrong, Stacey was pissed about her situation. She couldn't believe that she had to have so many surgeries and that her life would never be the same. But she always found a way to laugh and to make others laugh. We spent plenty of therapy sessions talking about men, tequila, and life in general. She was an expert in all of those areas. Her greatest hour was with her family; laughing, smiling and being funny.

Every year when I'm addressing my Christmas cards, I run across Stacey's address and my heart aches that she left us so young. I am glad that I got to know such a wonderful, loving person.

Susan Luce

Jill's Memory

When I read this clever book and look at all the memorable pictures of Stacey, I began to reflect upon the many wonderful experiences we shared through the years. Stacey and I, along with our brother Andy, had a love of humor and laughter which we often shared as a family. There are so many stories of Stacey and me that flood my mind. Thinking of them always makes me smile!

Stacey was seven years older than me. As I approached my teenage years, she and I became closer; it was much easier to relate to one another. From that point on, I always remember Stacey being a pillar of support. Whether I needed a place to crash, a creative idea or advice on how to deal with a problem; she listened, she yelled (sometimes), she laughed and she was truthful. I always felt lucky to have a big sis that I could trust, enjoy and laugh with.

When I turned 16, I was beyond excited to get my driver's license. My Mom wasn't able to take me to motor vehicles, so Stacey offered to take me. When we got there we were told we couldn't use Stacey's car for the exam because her car was missing the front license plate. Stacey wasn't the most patient person (neither am I), so after a few hundred curse words, we drove the car to a gas station. We asked the attendant to help put the front plate on the car. We waited a few minutes and before he could finish, he asked us to pull the car up so another car could squeeze around us. What we didn't realize was that when we pulled the car up we ran over the license plate! The attendant came out to finish the job but couldn't find the plate. After about ten minutes of looking and another 300 curse words and several dirty looks from my sister, we realized what had happened. So Stacey slowly backed up and as we looked in front of the car, there was the missing plate! Once we both got in the car to head back to motor vehicles, we looked at one another and just cracked up. I passed the test that day but passing the test really isn't the memory that I recall. It is the memory of Stacey taking me for this very important milestone, cursing up a storm when things didn't go our way, and of course, letting me not only drive home but use her car for the entire week!

My sister was a real character with a heart of gold and a zest for life.

Jillian

Dear Stacey,

I want you to know that we all miss you terribly! Jill always makes sure that we continue to celebrate together on your birthday. But of course you already know that!

I think of you and remember all the wonderful times we had together. When you heard that Shawn wanted a Monopoly theme for his Bar Mitzvah you called us to offer your creative talents. Seeing what you had accomplished, it was evident that you had given 100% of your time and creative talent. You always put your heart and soul into every project, which was greatly appreciated... and still is.

I remember visiting you in the hospital when you had that painful surgery after you broke your arm. Even though you had metal pins sticking out of your arm and shoulder and were visibly in pain, when I walked into your room you were concerned about me and my back issues.

You are the one who told me which surgeon was the best, and as usual, you were right! We truly bonded while healing together, whether it was sharing our surgery experiences or our late night talks at Structure House.

When Jillian found your outline for a book to share your "hospital wisdom" from experience, we were so excited! I will always be so grateful to Jill for giving me the opportunity to work on your project and help bring it to fruition.

I know you wanted the title to be A HOSPITAL HANDBOOK FOR DUMMIES, but we changed it because you ARE our Guardian Angel and you lived in apartment 1111. My parents, your Aunt Rose and Uncle Julie, lived in that same apartment before they passed away. I was so happy you moved in and I know my parents were as well. You even painted a long stem rose over the closet door, which gave me a true sense of peace. I always felt their energy when I walked into #1111. I know you did as well!

I often see images of you with your mischievous smile and definitely feel your presence. We know we are receiving your signs when we see the number 1111 on a license plate or when we happen to glance at the clock and the time is 11:11. Soon after you left us we began to experience beautiful blue butterflies flying freely around us. I want you to know that we feel your energy and spirit and we hope you feel our love.

Now you are in heaven and finally free of pain, which gives us great comfort. I truly wish I could get one last hug from you, but I will settle for a blue butterfly!

Love forever and beyond,
Aunt Ilene xo